Hide and Seek

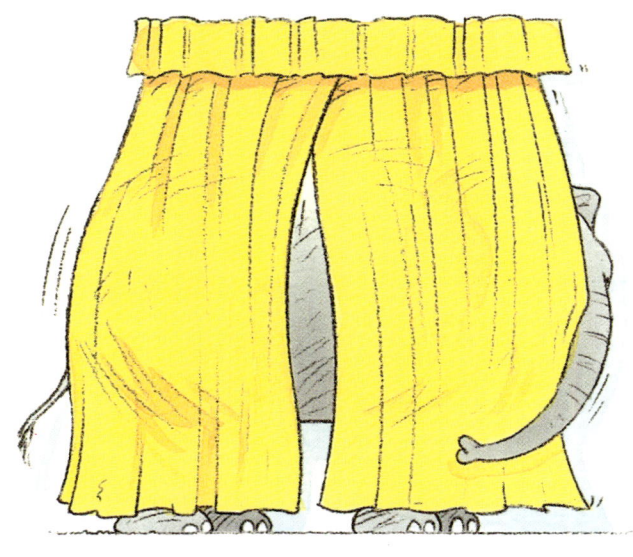

Story by Teresa Heapy
Illustrations by Stuart Trotter

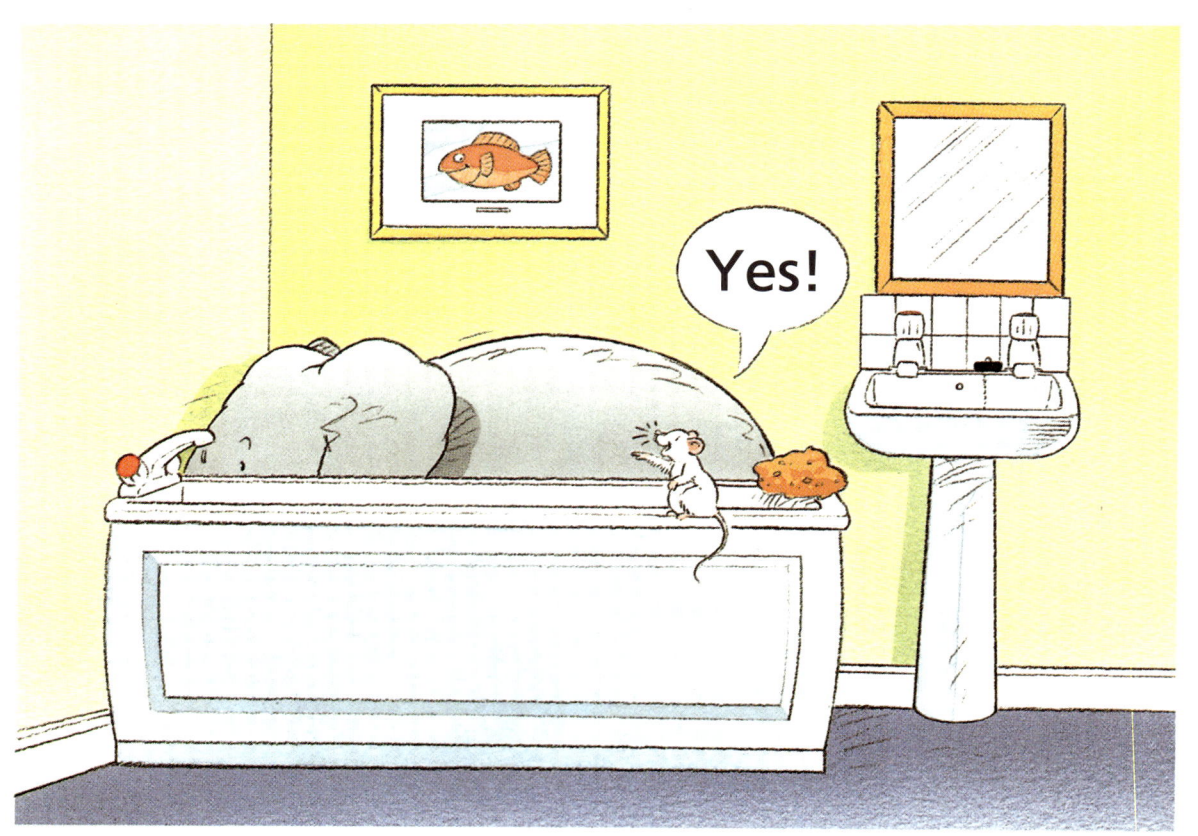

Is she in the bathroom?

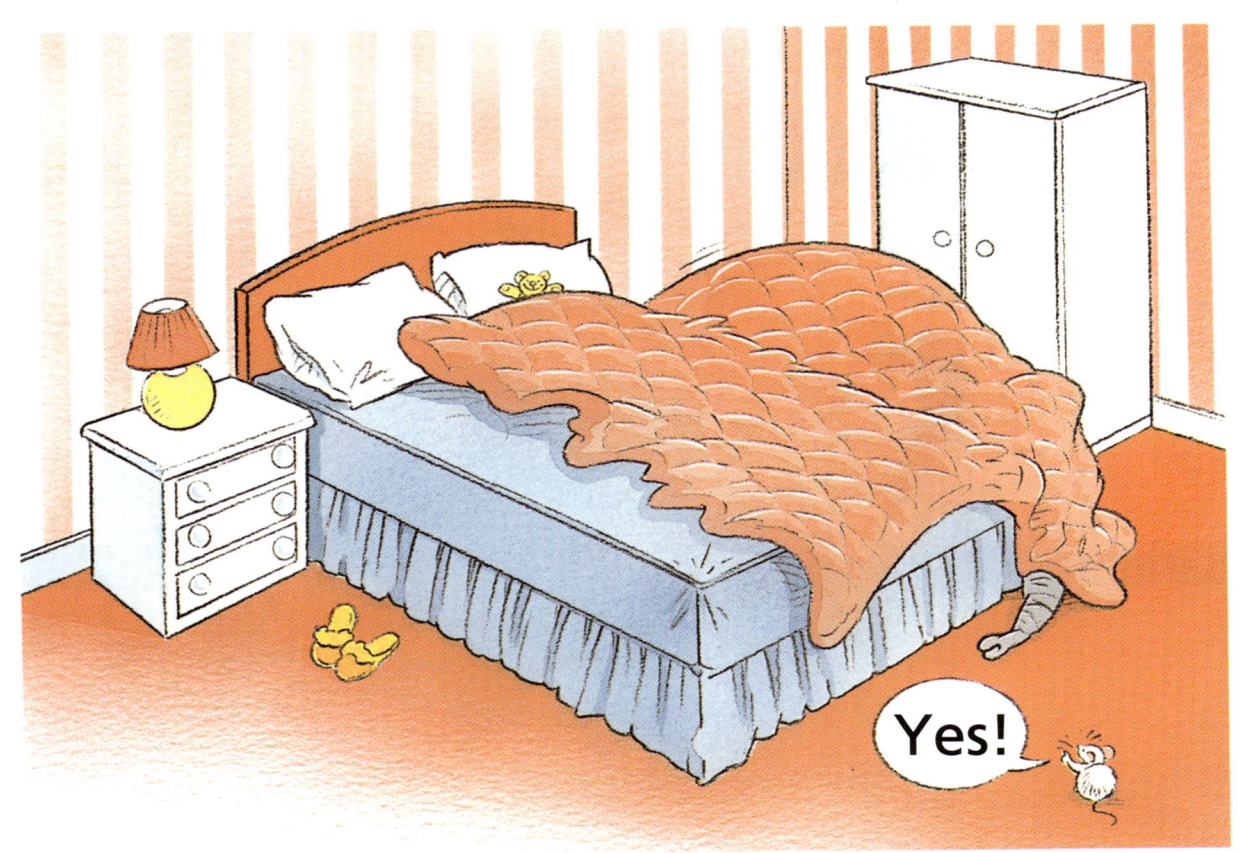

Is she in the bedroom?

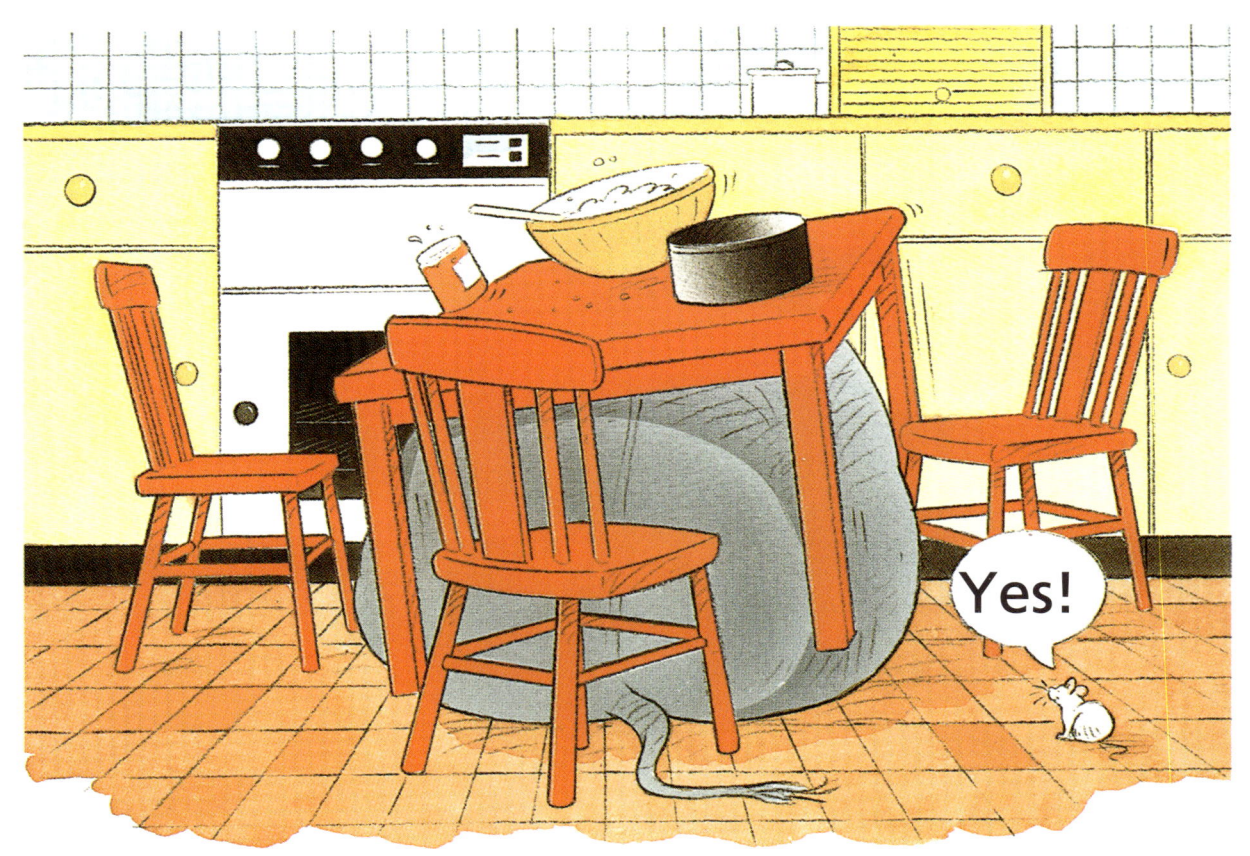

Is she in the kitchen?

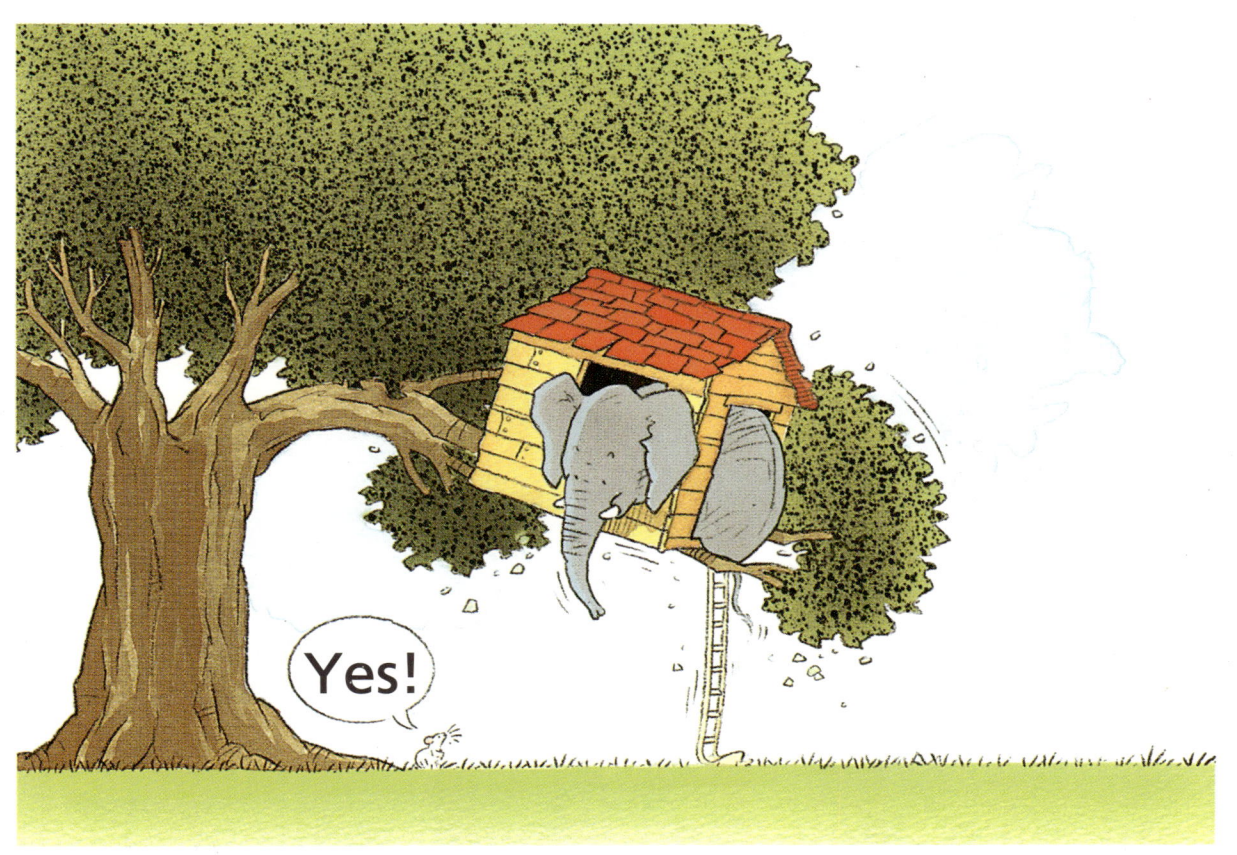

Is she in the tree house?

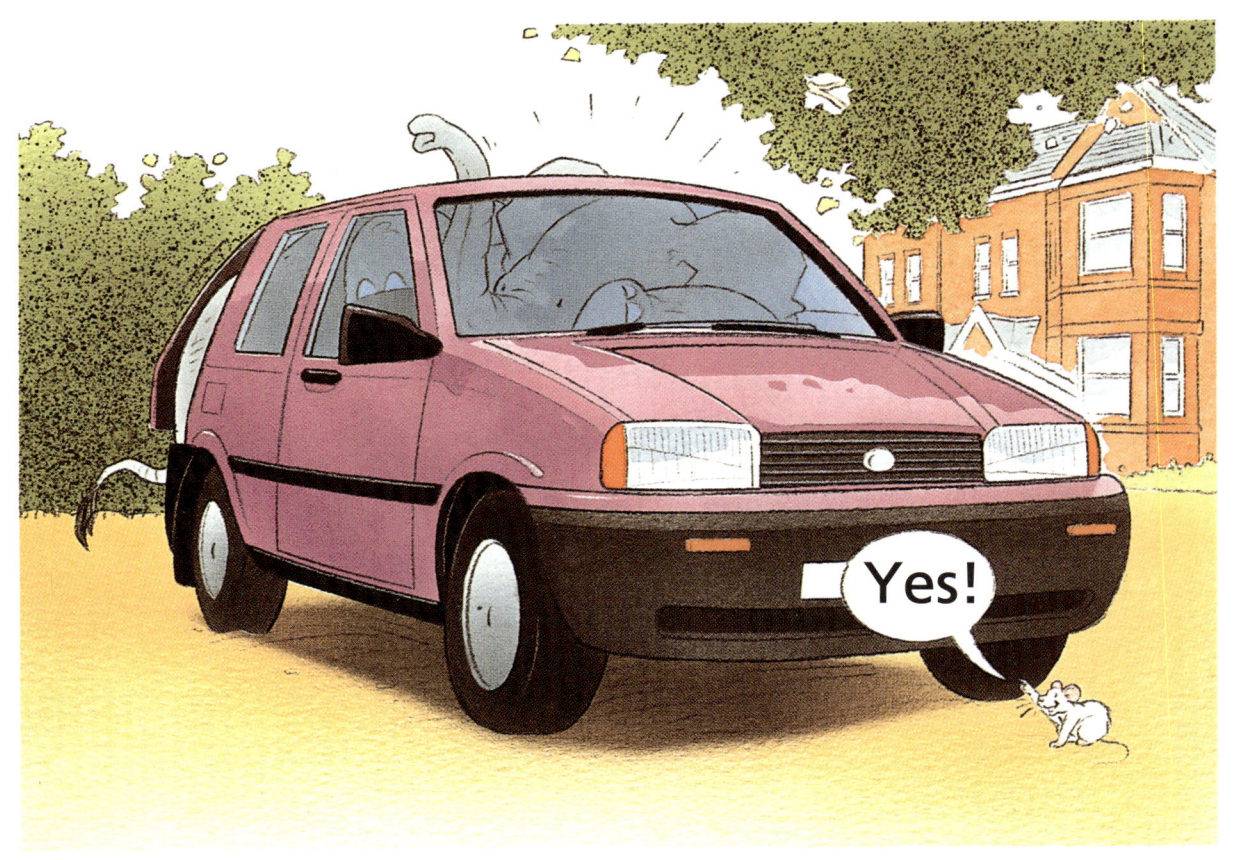

Is she in the car?

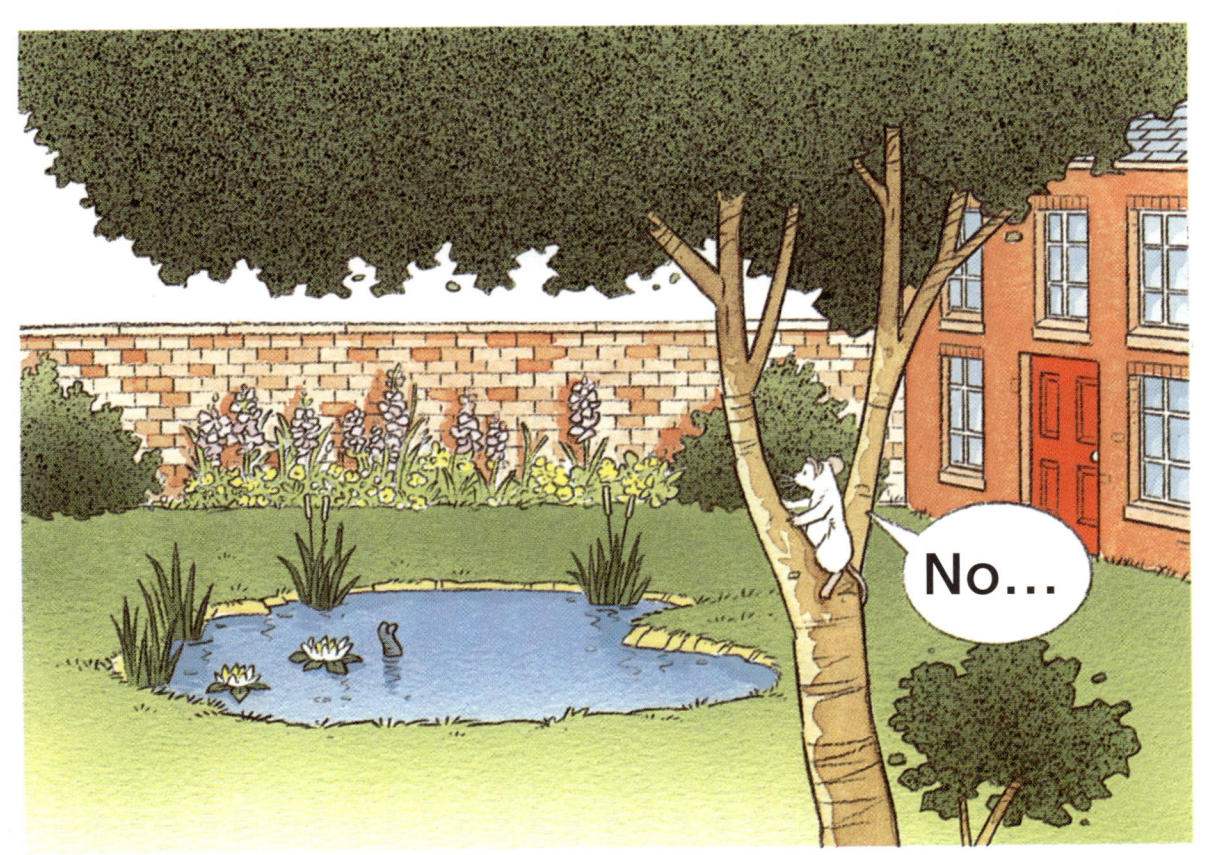

Is she in the garden?

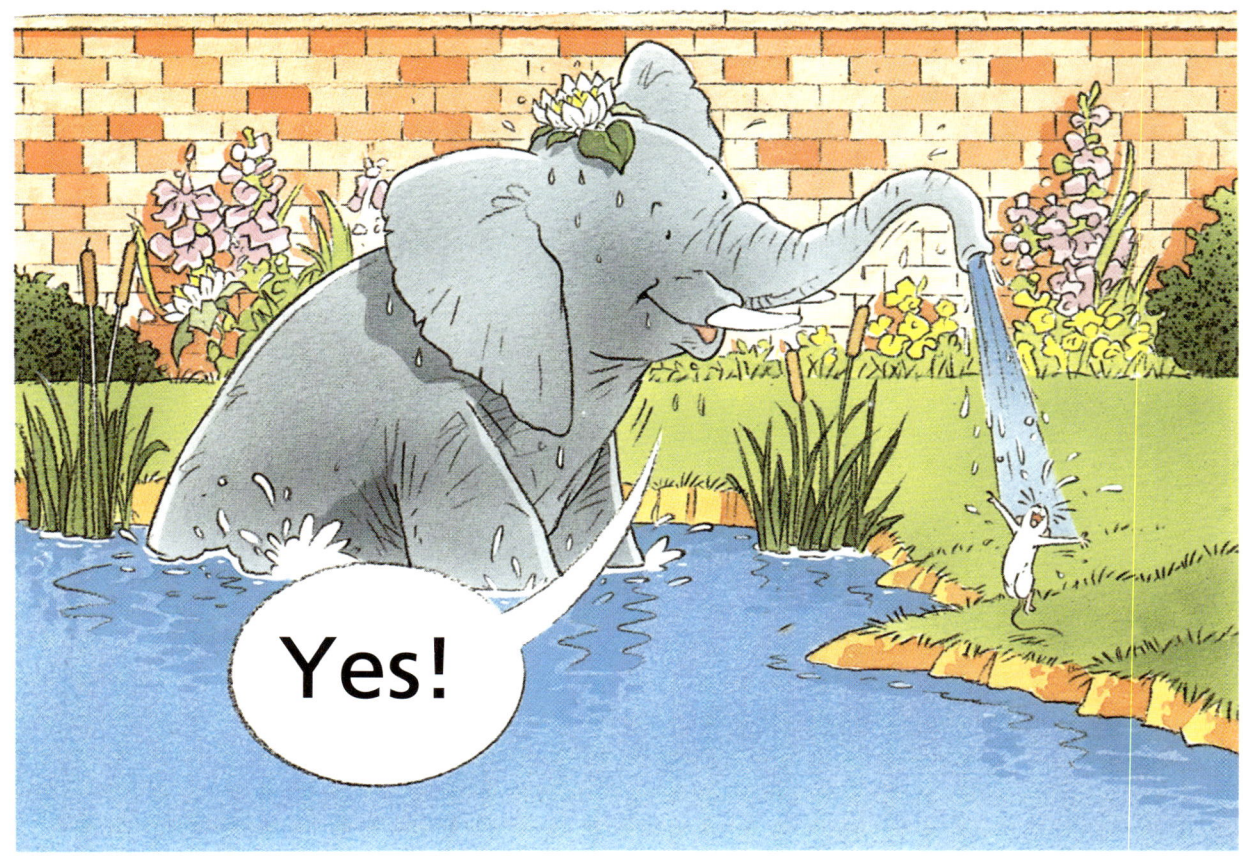